Quic

Vegan Desse   k

Over 80 delicious recipes for c..cs, cupcakes, brownies, cookies, fudge, pies, candy, and so much more!

By Susan Evans

Other popular books by Susan Evans

Vegetarian Slow Cooker Cookbook:
Over 75 recipes for meals, soups, stews, desserts, and sides

Quick & Easy Asian Vegetarian Cookbook:
Over 50 recipes for stir fries, rice, noodles, and appetizers

Vegetarian Mediterranean Cookbook:
Over 50 recipes for appetizers, salads, dips, and main dishes

Quick & Easy Vegetarian Rice Cooker Meals:
Over 50 recipes for breakfast, main dishes, and desserts

Quick & Easy Rice Cooker Meals:
Over 60 recipes for breakfast, main dishes, soups, and desserts

Quick & Easy Microwave Meals:
Over 50 recipes for breakfast, snacks, meals and desserts

Halloween Cookbook:
80 Ghoulish recipes for appetizers, meals, drinks, and desserts

FREE BONUS!

Would you like to receive one of my cookbooks for free? Just leave me on honest review on Amazon and I will send you a digital version of the cookbook of your choice! All you have to do is email me proof of your review and the desired cookbook and format to susan.evans.author@gmail.com. Thank you for your support, and have fun cooking!

SNACKS & APPETIZERS 83

THANK YOU 97

INTRODUCTION

Being on a vegan diet doesn't mean cutting cookies, brownies, cakes, and pies out of your life. However, desserts are intimidating to prepare when you are new to cooking and recipes without butter, eggs, and milk are hard to find. This cookbook contains over eighty deceptively simple recipes will guide you through decadent vegan desserts great for dinners, birthday parties, or for a bit of self-indulgence. Whatever the occasion, you'll find deliciously rich vegan desserts that even your omnivores will drool over.

Depriving yourself of chocolate is also not part of a vegan diet. You will notice that some of the following recipes require chocolate chips or cocoa powder. Make sure the product you are buying is dark chocolate or vegan milk chocolate. Many good-quality chocolates are naturally vegan and don't contain any animal products at all. However, not all companies mark their product as vegan, so ensure the chocolate or cocoa powder you are buying does not contain milk, milk fat, butter fat, or other animal ingredients. Now let's satisfy your sweet tooth and prepare some delicious vegan desserts!

MEASUREMENT CONVERSIONS

Liquid/Volume Measurements (approximate)

1 teaspoon = 1/6 fluid ounce (oz.) = 1/3 tablespoon = 5 ml

1 tablespoon = 1/2 fluid ounce (oz.) = 3 teaspoons = 15 ml

1 fluid ounce (oz.) = 2 tablespoons = 1/8 cup = 30 ml

1/4 cup = 2 fluid ounces (oz.) = 4 tablespoons = 60 ml

1/3 cup = 2⅔ fluid ounces (oz.) = 5 ⅓ tablespoons = 80 ml

1/2 cup = 4 fluid ounces (oz.) = 8 tablespoons = 120 ml

2/3 cup = 5⅓ fluid ounces (oz.) = 10⅔ tablespoons = 160 ml

3/4 cup = 6 fluid ounces (oz.) = 12 tablespoons = 180 ml

7/8 cup = 7 fluid ounces (oz.) = 14 tablespoons = 210 ml

1 cup = 8 fluid ounces (oz.) = 1/2 pint = 240 ml

1 pint = 16 fluid ounces (oz.) = 2 cups = 1/2 quart = 475 ml

1 quart = 4 cups = 32 fluid ounces (oz.) = 2 pints = 950 ml

1 liter = 1.055 quarts = 4.22 cups = 2.11 pints = 1000 ml

1 gallon = 4 quarts = 8 pints = 3.8 liters

Dry/Weight Measurements (approximate)

1 ounce (oz.) = 30 grams (g)

2 ounces (oz.) = 55 grams (g)

3 ounces (oz.) = 85 grams (g)

1/4 pound (lb.) = 4 ounces (oz.) = 125 grams (g)

1/2 pound (lb.) = 8 ounces (oz.) = 240 grams (g)

3/4 pound (lb.) = 12 ounces (oz.) = 375 grams (g)

1 pound (lb.) = 16 ounces (oz.) = 455 grams (g)

2 pounds (lbs.) = 32 ounces (oz.) = 910 grams (g)

1 kilogram (kg) = 2.2 pounds (lbs.) = 1000 gram (g)

C<small>AKES</small> & C<small>UPCAKES</small>

Vanilla Cake

SERVINGS: 8
PREP TIME: 15 min.
TOTAL TIME: 50 min.

Ingredients

- 1 cup plain soy milk
- 1 tablespoon apple cider vinegar
- 1½ cups unbleached all-purpose flour
- 1 cup white sugar
- 1 teaspoon baking soda
- 1 teaspoon baking powder
- 1/2 teaspoon salt
- 1/3 cup canola oil
- 1/4 cup water
- 1 tablespoon lemon juice
- 1 tablespoon vanilla extract
- 1/4 teaspoon almond extract

Instructions

1. Preheat oven to 350 degrees F (175 degrees C). Grease and sprinkle flour an 8 x 8-inch baking dish.
2. Combine soy milk and vinegar together in large measuring cup.
3. Whisk the flour, sugar, baking soda, baking powder, and salt in a bowl.
4. In the soy milk mixture, mix canola oil, water, lemon juice, vanilla extract, and almond extract using a fork. Stir soy milk mixture into flour mixture until there are no lumps. Pour batter into the baking dish.
5. Bake in the preheated oven for about 30 minutes or until a toothpick inserted in the center of the cake comes out clean.

Cherry Cheesecake

SERVINGS: 4
PREP TIME: 10 min.
TOTAL TIME: 2 hours 50 min

Ingredients

- 2 cups graham cracker crumbs
- 1/4 cup real maple syrup
- 1 (8 oz.) package firm silken tofu
- 1 (8 oz.) container non-dairy cream cheese
- 1 tablespoon lemon zest
- 1½ lemons, juiced
- 1 cup confectioners' sugar
- 1 tablespoon cornstarch
- 2 tablespoons soy milk
- 1 (21 oz.) can cherry pie filling

Instructions

1. Preheat oven to 350 degrees F (175 degrees C).
2. In a medium bowl, combine graham cracker crumbs and 1/4 cup maple syrup. Press the mixture in a 9-inch pie tin and bake for 5 minutes.
3. Using a blender, mix the tofu, vegan cream cheese, lemon zest and juice, and confectioners' sugar. Dissolve corn-starch in the soy milk, and add to blender. Blend until smooth. Pour into the baked crust.
4. Bake at 350 degrees F (175 degrees C) for 25 minutes. Reduce heat to 325 degrees F (165 degrees C), and continue baking for 15 minutes. Cool on a wire rack, and refrigerate for several hours.
5. Invert on a plate, and invert once more on a serving platter. Pour the cherry pie filling over the top. Serve.

Coconut Muffins
SERVINGS: 33
PREP TIME: 10 min.
TOTAL TIME: 40 min.

Ingredients

- 2½ cups coconut milk
- 1 tablespoon water
- 1¼ cups white rice flour
- 2 cups shredded unsweetened coconut
- 1 teaspoon salt
- 1 tablespoon white sugar

Instructions

1. Preheat oven to 375 degrees F (190 degrees C). Spray mini muffin pan with cooking spray.
2. In a mixing bowl, mix the coconut milk with the water. Add and stir in white rice flour, shredded coconut, and salt. Spoon this mixture into the muffin pan, and sprinkle with sugar.
3. Bake in the preheated oven for about 30 minutes or until the tops are golden brown and crusty.

Rum and Chocolate Cheesecake

SERVINGS: 12
PREP TIME: 30 min.
TOTAL TIME: 3 hours

Ingredients

- 1 cup ground almonds
- 1 cup whole wheat flour
- 2/3 cup vegan margarine
- 2 (12 oz.) packages firm tofu
- 1½ cups demerara sugar
- 7 tablespoons unsweetened cocoa powder
- 1/4 cup sunflower seed oil
- 1/2 cup soy milk
- 1/4 cup dark rum
- 1½ teaspoons vanilla extract

Instructions

1. Preheat oven to 325 degrees F (165 degrees C) Combine ground almonds and whole wheat flour in a medium bowl. Add in margarine until a dough is formed. In a 9-inch spring form pan, press dough into the bottom and half-way up the sides.
2. Crumble the tofu in a blender. Add sugar, cocoa, oil, soy milk, rum and vanilla. Blend until smooth and creamy. Pour into crust.
3. Bake in the preheated oven for 75 minutes or until filling is set. Allow to cool on a rack and then chill thoroughly in refrigerator for at least 90 minutes.

Chocolate Cupcakes with Almond Butter Cream

SERVINGS: 11-12
PREP/TOTAL TIME: 30 min.

Ingredients

For cupcakes

- 1 cup vanilla almond milk
- 1 cup sugar
- 1/3 cup extra virgin olive oil
- 1 tablespoon apple cider vinegar
- 1 tablespoon pure vanilla extract
- 1/2 teaspoon pure almond extract
- 1½ cups unbleached all-purpose flour
- 1/3 cup cocoa powder, sifted
- 1 teaspoon baking soda
- 3/4 teaspoon kosher salt, to taste

For the butter cream

- 1/2 cup vegan butter stick, room temperature
- 3 cups icing sugar, sifted
- 1/2 teaspoon kosher salt
- 1 teaspoon pure almond extract
- 1.5-2 tablespoon non-dairy milk

Instructions

1. Preheat oven to 350 degrees F and line a cupcake pan with paper liners. In a large bowl, beat the non-dairy milk, oil, sugar, apple cider vinegar, vanilla, almond extract, using an electric mixer on medium speed for one or two minutes.
2. Sift in the flour, cocoa powder, baking soda, and salt. Mix well, until smooth.

3. Spoon the batter into prepared pan, about two thirds full for each. Bake at 350 degrees F for about 22 minutes, or until the cupcake springs back when lightly pressed. Allow to completely cool.
4. In a mixing bowl, beat 1/2 cup of the vegan butter with an electric mixer. Add in and mix the milk, extract, and salt. Gradually add the icing sugar, mixing slowly until fully combined. Mix for about 5-10 minutes or until fluffy.
5. Frost cooled cupcakes. Serve.

Brownie Cupcakes
SERVINGS: 24
PREP TIME: 15 min.
TOTAL TIME: 1 hour

Ingredients

- 2¼ cups whole wheat flour
- 2 cups brown sugar
- 1 cup unsweetened cocoa powder
- 2 teaspoons baking soda
- 1 teaspoon salt
- 1½ cups water
- 1 over-ripe banana, mashed
- 1/2 cup canola oil
- 4 teaspoons apple cider vinegar
- 1/2 cup chocolate chips
- 1 cup chunky peanut butter
- 1/3 cup margarine, melted
- 1/3 cup coconut milk
- 1 teaspoon vanilla extract
- 1 cup confectioners' sugar

Instructions

1. Preheat oven to 350 degrees F (175 degrees C). Line 24 muffin cups with paper liners or grease and flour.
2. In a large bowl, whisk whole wheat flour, brown sugar, cocoa powder, and salt together.
3. Add water, banana, canola oil, and apple cider vinegar to flour mixture and blend until smooth. Stir in chocolate chips. Pour this batter into the prepared muffin cups.
4. Bake in the preheated oven 15 to 20 minutes or until tops are golden. Transfer cupcakes to wire racks and cool.
5. With a mixer, beat peanut butter and margarine together in a bowl. Add coconut milk and vanilla. Gradually beat confectioners' sugar this mixture until well mixed.
6. Top cupcakes with icing

Gluten-Free Gingerbread Cake

SERVINGS: 24
PREP TIME: 15 min.
TOTAL TIME: 50 min

Ingredients

- 1 cup amaranth flour
- 1 cup buckwheat flour
- 1/2 cup coconut flour
- 2½ teaspoons baking soda
- 2 teaspoons ground cinnamon
- 2 teaspoons ground ginger
- 1/2 teaspoon ground cloves
- 1/2 teaspoon ground nutmeg
- 1/2 teaspoon salt
- 2 tablespoons flax seed meal
- 6 tablespoons water
- 3/4 cup agave nectar
- 3/4 cup canola oil
- 3/4 cup molasses
- 2 teaspoons grated fresh ginger
- 1 teaspoon lemon zest, or more to taste
- 1 cup boiling water

Instructions

1. Preheat oven to 350 degrees F (175 degrees C). Grease a 9 x 13-inch baking pan.
2. In a large bowl, mix the amaranth flour, buckwheat flour, coconut flour, baking soda, cinnamon, ground ginger, cloves, nutmeg, and salt together in a large bowl. Bore a hole in the center of the flour mixture.
3. In a separate bowl, stir flax meal and 6 tablespoons water together. Add agave nectar, canola oil, molasses, grated fresh ginger, and lemon zest, and stir. Pour wet ingredients into the well in the flour mixture and mix well. Slowly stir boiling water into the batter until fully incorporated. Pour this batter into the prepared baking pan.

4. Bake in the preheated oven 35-40 minutes or until a toothpick inserted into the center of the cake comes out clean.

Carrot Cake

SERVINGS: 24
PREP TIME: 15 min.
TOTAL TIME: 3 hours

Ingredients

- 2 cups whole wheat flour
- 1/4 cup soy flour (optional)
- 1½ tablespoons ground cinnamon
- 1 tablespoon ground cloves
- 4 teaspoons baking soda
- 2 teaspoons tapioca starch (optional)
- 1/2 teaspoon salt
- 1½ cups hot water
- 1/4 cup flax seed meal
- 2 cups packed brown sugar
- 4 teaspoons vanilla extract
- 3/4 cup dried currants (optional)
- 6 carrots, grated
- 1/2 cup blanched slivered almonds

Instructions

1. Preheat oven to 350 degrees F (175 degrees C). Spray a 9x13 inch baking pan with cooking spray. In a bowl, whisk the whole wheat flour, soy flour, cinnamon, ground cloves, baking soda, tapioca starch, and salt until blended. Set aside.
2. Pour the hot water into a mixing bowl, and dust with the flax meal. Stir for a minute until the flax starts to absorb the water, and mixture slightly thickens. Stir in the brown sugar and vanilla until the sugar has dissolved, then add the currants, carrots, and almonds. Stir the dry mixture until just moistened, then pour into the prepared pan.
3. Bake in the preheated oven about 30 minutes or until a toothpick inserted into the center comes out clean. Cool in the pan for 10 minutes. Remove to cool completely on a wire rack.

Chocolate Cake

SERVINGS: 8
PREP TIME: 15 min.
TOTAL TIME: 1 hour

Ingredients

- 1½ cup all-purpose flour
- 1 cup white sugar
- ¼ cup cocoa powder
- 1 teaspoon baking soda
- ½ teaspoon salt
- 1/3 cup vegetable oil
- 1 teaspoon vanilla extract
- 1 teaspoon distilled white vinegar
- 1 cup water

Instructions

1. Preheat oven to 375°F. Lightly grease one 9 x 5-inch pan.
2. Combine the flour, sugar, cocoa, baking soda and salt. Add the oil, vanilla, vinegar and water. Mix until smooth. Pour into prepared pan.
3. Bake at 375°F for 45 minutes or until set. Remove from oven and cool.

Grannie's Cupcakes

SERVINGS: 18
PREP TIME: 10 min.
TOTAL TIME: 25min.

Ingredients

- 1 tablespoon apple cider vinegar
- 1½ cups almond milk
- 2 cups all-purpose flour
- 1 cup white sugar
- 2 teaspoons baking powder
- 1/2 teaspoon baking soda
- 1/2 cup coconut oil, warmed until liquid
- 1¼ teaspoons vanilla extract

Instructions

1. Preheat oven to 350 degrees F. Line two 12 cup muffin pans with 18 paper baking cups, or grease.
2. In a cup, combine the vinegar with almond milk. Let stand until curdled, about 5 minutes.
3. In a large bowl, whisk the flour, sugar, baking powder, baking soda and salt. In a separate bowl, whisk the almond milk mixture, coconut oil and vanilla. Combine the wet ingredients with the dry ingredients and stir until blended. Pour the batter into the prepared cups, dividing evenly.
4. Bake in the preheated oven, 15 to 20 minutes or until the tops spring back when lightly pressed. Cool in the pan over a wire rack.
5. Frost with desired frosting and serve.

Orange Cake
SERVINGS: 16
PREP TIME: 15 min.
TOTAL TIME: 45 min.

Ingredients

- 1 large orange, peeled or 1 cup of orange juice
- 1½ cups all-purpose flour
- 1 cup white sugar
- 1/2 cup vegetable oil
- 1½ teaspoons baking soda
- 1/4 teaspoon salt

Instructions

1. Preheat oven to 375 degrees F (190 degrees C). Grease an 8 x 8-inch baking pan.
2. Blend the orange in a blender until it has liquefied. Measure 1 cup of orange juice. (Or just use 1 cup of store bought orange juice).
3. In a bowl, whisk the orange juice, flour, sugar, vegetable oil, baking soda, and salt. Pour this batter into prepared pan.
4. Bake in the preheated oven about 30 minutes or until a toothpick inserted in the center comes out clean.

Blonde Pumpkin Pie Browni

SERVINGS: 36
PREP TIME: 10 min.
TOTAL TIME: 30 min.

Ingredients

- 2 cups all-purpose flour
- 1/2 cup white sugar
- 1/4 cup brown sugar
- 1 teaspoon baking powder
- 1 teaspoon baking soda
- 1/2 teaspoon ground cinnamon
- 1/4 teaspoon ground cloves
- 1/4 teaspoon ground ginger
- 1/4 teaspoon ground nutmeg
- 1/4 teaspoon salt
- 1 (15 oz.) can pumpkin puree
- 1/4 cup canola oil
- 1 tablespoon vanilla extract

Instructions

1. Preheat oven to 375 degrees F (190 degrees C). Lightly grease a 9-inch square baking pan.
2. Sieve the flour, white sugar, brown sugar, baking powder, baking soda, cinnamon, cloves, ginger, nutmeg, and salt together in a bowl. Add and stir the pumpkin, canola oil, and vanilla extract into flour mixture until the batter thickens. Pour into prepared baking pan.
3. Bake in the preheated oven around 20 minutes or until a toothpick inserted in the center comes out clean.

Tofu Cheesecake

SERVINGS: 8
PREP TIME: 10 min.
TOTAL TIME: 2 hours 30 min.

Ingredients

- 2 (12 oz.) packages extra firm tofu, drained and cubed
- 1 cup white sugar
- 1 teaspoon vanilla extract
- 1/4 teaspoon salt
- 1/4 cup vegetable oil
- 2 tablespoons lemon juice
- 1 (9 inch) prepared graham cracker crust

Instructions

1. Preheat an oven to 350 degrees F (175 degrees C).
2. In a blender, mix the tofu, sugar, vanilla, salt, vegetable oil, and lemon juice. Blend until smooth. Pour into graham cracker pie crust.
3. Bake at 350 degrees F (175 degrees C) for 20 to 30 minutes or until set. Remove from oven and allow to cool. Refrigerate until chilled.

COOKIES

Oatmeal Chia Seed Cookies

SERVINGS: 12
PREP TIME: 15 min.
TOTAL TIME: 25 min.

Ingredients

- 2 cups rolled oats
- 1 cup brown sugar
- 2/3 cup whole wheat flour
- 2 tablespoons chia seeds
- 1 teaspoon ground cinnamon
- 1 teaspoon baking soda
- 1/2 teaspoon baking powder
- 1/2 teaspoon salt
- 2/3 cup applesauce
- 3 tablespoons coconut oil
- 1 cup dried cranberries
- 1/2 cup chocolate chips
- 1/4 cup shredded unsweetened coconut

Instructions

1. Preheat oven to 350 degrees F. Line a baking sheet with parchment paper.
2. In a bowl, combine oats, brown sugar, flour, chia seeds, cinnamon, baking soda, baking powder, and salt. Add in and stir applesauce and coconut oil until evenly mixed. Fold in cranberries, chocolate chips, and coconut into the dough mixture. Spoon onto the prepared baking sheet.
3. Bake in the preheated oven, 10 to 15 minutes or until edges of cookies are lightly browned.

Peanut Butter Balls (Gluten-Free)

SERVINGS: 16-20
PREP TIME: 15 min.
TOTAL TIME: 40 min.

Ingredients

- 1 cup 100% natural peanut butter (smooth or crunchy)
- 3½-4 tablespoons pure maple syrup, to taste
- 2-3 tablespoons coconut flour
- 1/4 teaspoon fine grain sea salt
- 6 tablespoons gluten-free rice crisp cereal
- 3/4 cup dark chocolate chips
- 1/2 tablespoon coconut oil

Instructions

1. Begin by stirring the jar of peanut butter very well. In a large bowl, mix the peanut butter and maple syrup vigorously, for 30-60 seconds or until it thickens.
2. Stir in the coconut flour. Let sit for a couple minutes to firm up. Add some more coconut flour if necessary, or add more syrup if it's too dry.
3. Add salt in the cereal and stir.
4. Shape into small balls.
5. In a small pot, add the chocolate chips and coconut oil and heat over low heat, stir frequently. Once half the chips have melted, remove from heat and stir until smooth.
6. With a fork, dip the balls into the melted chocolate. Place ball on a plate or cutting board lined with parchment. Repeat for all the balls. Set aside leftover chocolate.
7. Place balls in the freezer for 6-8 minutes or until mostly firm.
8. Dip a fork into the leftover melted chocolate and drizzle it on top of the balls to create a fancy design.
9. Freeze the balls for 10-15 minutes or until the chocolate is completely set.

Energy Cookies

Ingredients

- 4 cups rolled oats
- 1 (15 oz.) can cannellini beans, drained and rinsed
- 1/2 cup white sugar
- 1/2 cup brown sugar
- 1 teaspoon vanilla extract
- 1 teaspoon baking powder
- 1 teaspoon baking soda
- 1 teaspoon ground cinnamon
- 1/2 cup chopped pitted dates
- 1/2 cup flaked coconut
- 1/2 cup raisins
- 1/2 cup chopped walnuts

Instructions

1. Preheat the oven to 325 degrees F (165 degrees C). Grease cookie sheets.
2. Grind oats in a blender until resembling coarse flour.
3. Mash beans in a medium bowl until it is a smooth paste. Add and stir in the white sugar, brown sugar and vanilla until well blended.
4. Combine the ground oats, baking powder, baking soda and cinnamon. Blend into the bean mixture. Stir in the dates, coconut, raisins and walnuts. Drop large spoonfuls of dough onto the prepared cookie sheet.
5. Bake in the preheated oven for 10 to 15 minutes or until golden.
6. Cool on baking sheets for 5 minutes then remove to wire racks until completely cooled.

Banana Cookies

SERVINGS: 36
PREP TIME: 15 min.
TOTAL TIME: 50 min.

Ingredients

- 3 ripe bananas
- 2 cups rolled oats
- 1 cup dates, pitted and chopped
- 1/3 cup vegetable oil
- 1 teaspoon vanilla extract

Instructions

1. Preheat oven to 350 degrees F (175 degrees C).
2. Mash the bananas in a large bowl. Mix in oats, dates, oil, and vanilla, and allow to sit for 15 minutes. On an ungreased cookie sheet, drop teaspoonfuls of the banana mixture.
3. Bake in the preheated oven for 20 minutes or until lightly brown.

Chocolate Chip Walnut Cookies

SERVINGS: 36
PREP TIME/TOTAL TIME: 45 min.

Ingredients

- 2 cups all-purpose flour
- 1/4 teaspoon ground cinnamon
- 1/4 cup shortening
- 1/4 cup margarine
- 3/4 cup confectioners' sugar
- 1 cup chopped walnuts
- 1 cup semisweet chocolate chips

Instructions

1. Combine and mix the flour and cinnamon. In a separate large bowl, mix together shortening, margarine and powdered sugar. Gradually add in the flour/cinnamon mixture. Fold chopped nuts into the dough.
2. On floured surface roll into 1/4-inch thickness. Cut out circles with a 2 inch round cookie cutter. Place 1 inch apart on ungreased cookie sheet.
3. Put chocolate chip in the center of each cookie.
4. Bake at 400 degrees F (205 degrees C) for 8-10 minutes or until lightly browned. Cool on wire racks.

Gluten Free Peppermint Patties

SERVINGS: 25
PREP TIME: 20 min.
TOTAL TIME: 1.5 hours

Ingredients

- 1/2 cup raw cashews, soaked
- 1/2 cup coconut oil, melted
- 3-4 tablespoons agave nectar, to taste
- 2 tablespoons almond milk
- 1 teaspoon peppermint extract
- 3/4 cup dark chocolate chips
- 1/2 tablespoon coconut oil

Instructions

1. Place cashews in a bowl and cover with water. Soak for 2-3 hours or overnight for best results.
2. Drain and rinse the cashews.
3. Combine cashews, melted coconut oil, agave, milk, and peppermint extract into a high-speed blender. Blend on high speed until smooth.
4. Line a baking sheet with parchment paper. Add a half tablespoon of filling into a mini cupcake/candy liners. Place on the baking sheet. Repeat until there is no more filling left. Freeze, uncovered, for 20-35 minutes, or until firm.
5. Take the patties out of the cupcake liners and set each on top of their liner. Return to the freezer for 10 minutes to firm up more.
6. Melt the chocolate and coconut oil in a small pot over low heat. When half of the chips are melted, remove from the heat and continue to stir until all the chips are melted. Allow chocolate to cool for a few minutes.
7. Remove patties from the freezer and with a fork, dunk them into the melted chocolate. Tap the side to shake off excess chocolate and place on parchment paper. Do this as quickly as possible so the patties don't melt. If chocolate thickens, reheat chocolate again over low heat.
8. Return patties to the freezer for about 10 minutes or until set and chocolate coating is firm.

No-Bake Oatmeal Chocolate Cookies

Ingredients

- 2/3 cup maple syrup
- 1/4 cup vegetable oil
- 5 tablespoons unsweetened cocoa powder
- 1 teaspoon ground cinnamon
- 1/2 cup peanut butter
- 1 cup rolled oats
- 1 teaspoon vanilla extract

Instructions

1. Over medium heat combine maple syrup, oil, cocoa and cinnamon in a saucepan. Boil for three minutes, while constantly stirring. Remove from heat and stir in the peanut butter, rolled oats and vanilla until it is well mixed.
2. Drop large spoonfuls onto waxed paper. Chill for about 30 minutes.

Roasted Almond Cookies

SERVINGS: 6
PREP TIME: 15 min.
TOTAL TIME: 1 hour 45 min

Ingredients

- 1 cup raw whole almonds
- 1 cup oat flour
- 1/2 cup real maple syrup
- 1 teaspoon almond extract

Instructions

1. Preheat oven to 275 degrees F (135 degrees C). Spread almonds onto a baking sheet. Toast in preheated oven for about 45 minutes or until nuts turn golden brown and become fragrant. Once toasted, remove from oven and cool to room temperature. Grind the almonds in a food processor.
2. Raise oven temperature to 350 degrees F (175 degrees C). Oil a baking sheet with vegetable oil.
3. Mix together ground almonds, oat flour, maple syrup, and almond extract in a bowl. Form this mixture into 6 balls, then flatten the balls into cookies about 1/4 inch thick. Place onto the prepared baking sheet.
4. Bake 12 to 15 minutes or until crisp and brown around the edges. Remove and allow to cool.

BROWNIES & FUDGE

Gluten-Free Brownies

SERVINGS: 12
PREP TIME: 20 min.
TOTAL TIME: 1 hour 5 min.

Ingredients

- 3 tablespoons chia seed meal
- 1/2 cup water
- 1 cup raw sugar
- 1/2 cup agave nectar
- 3 tablespoons vegan margarine
- 1 teaspoon gluten-free vanilla extract
- 3/4 cup brown rice flour
- 1/2 cup almond meal
- 1 teaspoon baking powder
- 1/2 teaspoon salt
- 3/4 cup cocoa powder

Instructions

1. Preheat oven to 350 degrees F (175 degrees C). Lightly oil a baking dish.
2. In bowl, beat the chia meal and water together in a bowl. Let stand about 5 minutes or until thick. With a blender, blend the raw sugar and agave into chia seed mixture. Add and blend vegan margarine and vanilla extract.
3. In a large bowl, mix brown rice flour, almond meal, baking powder, and salt. Add and stir the cocoa powder. Add the chia meal mixture and stir until combined. Pour into prepared baking dish.
4. Bake in the preheated oven, 45 to 55 minutes or until set and the top is dry.

Peanut Butter Fudge

SERVINGS: 24
PREP TIME: 10 min.
TOTAL TIME: 45 min.

Ingredients

- 3/4 cup vegan margarine
- 1 cup peanut butter
- 3 ⅔ cups confectioners' sugar

Instructions

1. Lightly grease a 9 x 9-inch baking dish.
2. Melt margarine in a saucepan over low heat. Remove from heat. Stir in peanut butter until smooth. Gradually add and stir confectioners' sugar, until well mixed.
3. Pour into prepared pan and chill until firm. Cut into squares and serve.

Peanut Butter Avocado Brownies

SERVINGS: 20
PREP TIME: 15 min.
TOTAL TIME: 1 hour 45 min.

Ingredients

- 1 cup natural creamy peanut butter
- 1 (12 oz.) bag chocolate chips
- 1½ cups white sugar
- 1 avocado, peeled and pitted
- 1/2 cup soy milk
- 1/2 cup canola oil
- 1 cup whole-wheat flour
- 1 teaspoon baking powder
- 1 teaspoon salt

Instructions

1. Preheat oven to 350 degrees F (175 degrees C). Grease a 9 x 13-inch baking pan.
2. Over low heat, melt peanut butter, chocolate chips, and sugar, constantly stirring, about 5 minutes. Increase heat to medium and continue stirring for about 5 more minutes or until mixture bubbles. Remove from heat.
3. Blend the avocado, soy milk, and canola oil in a food processor until smooth. Stir and combine avocado mixture into chocolate mixture.
4. In a large bowl, whisk flour, baking powder, and salt together until well mixed. Add avocado-chocolate mixture to the flour mixture and stir until combined. Pour batter into the prepared baking pan.
5. Bake in the preheated oven for about 20 minutes or until the edges are crisp. Cool brownies completely. Cut and serve.

Christmas Fudge

SERVINGS: 24
PREP TIME: 15 min.
TOTAL TIME: 50 min.

Ingredients

- 1/2 cup good-quality unsweetened cocoa powder
- 1/2 cup real maple syrup
- 1 teaspoon vanilla extract
- 1 pinch salt
- 1/2 cup refined coconut oil, melted
- 1/2 cup chopped walnuts
- 1 teaspoon unsweetened cocoa powder for dusting

Instructions

1. In a mixing bowl, stir in 1/2 cup cocoa powder, maple syrup, vanilla extract, and salt. Pour in melted coconut oil, stirring until thoroughly combined, coconut oil hardens, and the mixture becomes thick and grainy.
2. Place walnuts into a dry skillet over medium heat for 30 seconds to 1 minute; shaking skillet until walnuts are hot and aromatic. Turn off heat and let walnuts slightly cool, about 1 minute.
3. Stir warm walnuts into fudge and stir until smooth and glossy.
4. Pour fudge into a silicone ice cube mould. Scrape excess fudge back into the mixing bowl. Smooth the tops of the fudge pieces.
5. Wrap mould in plastic wrap and freeze, at least 30 minutes or until fudge is firm. Remove plastic wrap and remove each fudge piece out of the mould.
6. Dust pieces with 1 teaspoon cocoa powder before serving. Serve cold and freeze leftovers.

Vegan Brownies

SERVINGS: 16
PREP TIME: 15 min.
TOTAL TIME: 50 min.

Ingredients

- 2 cups unbleached all-purpose flour
- 2 cups white sugar
- 3/4 cup unsweetened cocoa powder
- 1 teaspoon baking powder
- 1 teaspoon salt
- 1 cup water
- 1 cup vegetable oil
- 1 teaspoon vanilla extract

Instructions

1. Preheat the oven to 350 degrees F (175 degrees C).
2. In a large bowl, stir flour, sugar, cocoa powder, baking powder and salt. Pour in water, vegetable oil and vanilla. Combine and mix until well blended. Spread flour mixture evenly on a 9 x13 inch baking pan.
3. Bake for 25 to 30 minutes in the preheated oven, until the top is not glossy anymore. Let cool for at least 10 minutes. Cut into squares and serve.

Banana Brownies
SERVINGS: 20
PREP TIME: 10 min.
TOTAL TIME: 40 min.

Ingredients

- 2 ripe bananas, mashed
- 1½ cups vegetable oil
- 1 cup potato flour
- 1 cup brown rice flour
- 2 cups white sugar
- 1/2 cup unsweetened cocoa powder
- 1/2 teaspoon baking soda
- 5/8 teaspoon cream of tartar
- 1½ teaspoons sea salt

Instructions

1. Preheat the oven to 325 degrees F (165 degrees C.) Grease a 9 x 13-inch baking dish.
2. Mix together the potato flour, rice flour, sugar, cocoa powder, baking soda, cream of tartar and salt in a large bowl. In a separate bowl, blend the banana and oil. Stir banana mixture into the dry ingredients until well mixed. Spread evenly in the bottom of the prepared pan.
3. Bake in the preheated oven for 20 to 25 minutes or until they appear dry on the top. Cool completely. Cut into squares and serve.

Peanut-Butter Chocolate Fudge

SERVINGS: 24
PREP TIME: 10 min.
TOTAL TIME: 6 hours 10 min.

Ingredients

- 1 cup semi-sweet chocolate chips
- 1 cup peanut butter
- 3/4 cup maple syrup

Instructions

1. In a double boiler, melt chocolate chips with the peanut butter and maple syrup boiler over medium heat. Stir continually until smooth.
2. Pour into a dish lined with parchment paper.
3. Refrigerate overnight. Cut and serve.

No-Bake Almond Chocolate Bars

SERVINGS: 16
PREP TIME: 20 min.
TOTAL TIME: 1 hours 30 min

Ingredients

Crust
- 1½ cup whole almonds
- 2 tablespoons coconut oil
- 2 tablespoons coconut nectar syrup
- 1 tablespoon almond butter or peanut butter
- 1/2 teaspoon cinnamon
- pinch of fine grain sea salt, to taste
Middle layer
- 2 medium ripe bananas, peeled
- 1/4 cup coconut oil, softened slightly
- 2 tablespoons almond butter or peanut butter
- 1 teaspoon pure vanilla extract
- pinch of fine grain sea salt, to taste
Chocolate drizzle
- 3 tablespoons mini dark chocolate chips
- 1/2 tablespoon coconut oil

Instructions

1. Line an 8-inch square pan with two pieces of parchment paper, one going each way.
2. In a food processor or blender, process the almonds until a fine crumb forms. Add the rest of the crust ingredients and process until thoroughly mixed. The mixture should stick together when pressed with your fingers. If not, add a splash of water and process again for a couple of seconds.
3. Pour the crust mixture into the prepared pan, pressing down firmly and smoothing evenly into the pan. Place in freezer and go to the next step.
4. Rinse the food processor or blender. Add all the middle layer ingredients into the processor and process until smooth. Remove crust from the freezer and pour this mixture on top. Smooth out.

Return to the freezer for at least 1-1½ hours or until the middle layer is very firm to the touch.

5. In a small pot, heat the chocolate and coconut oil on the lowest heat, and stir to combine. When half of the chips have melted, remove the pot from the heat and stir until completely melted.

6. Remove the bars from the freezer. Lift out of the pan and slice into squares. Spread the squares on a plate lined with parchment paper.

7. Drizzle on the melted chocolate and return bars to the freezer until the chocolate is firm.

8. Serve. Wrap leftovers and store in the freezer.

Masala Chai Brownies

SERVINGS: 9
PREP TIME: 10 min.
TOTAL TIME: 1 hour 30 min.

Ingredients

- 2 tablespoons unsweetened cocoa powder
- 1/3 cup unsweetened shredded coconut
- 1 cup all-purpose flour
- 1 cup white sugar
- 1/4 cup unsweetened cocoa powder
- 1/2 teaspoon baking powder
- 1/2 teaspoon salt
- 1/2 cup very strongly brewed masala chai
- 1/2 cup canola oil
- 1/2 teaspoon vanilla extract

Instructions

1. Preheat an oven to 350 degrees F (175 degrees C). Spray an 8 x 8-inch baking pan with cooking spray. Lightly dust with the 2 tablespoons cocoa powder.
2. Place the coconut in the jar of a blender, pulsing to mince. Set aside.
3. Whisk flour, sugar, 1/4 cup cocoa powder, baking powder, and salt. Stir in the brewed chai, canola oil, and vanilla extract, until mixture is moistened. Fold in the coconut. Spread the batter in the prepared pan.
4. Bake in the preheated oven, about 20 minutes or until the top is no longer shiny. Allow to cool for 1 hour. Cut into squares and serve.

Tofu Triple Chocolate Brownies

SERVINGS: 12
PREP TIME: 20 min.
TOTAL TIME: 2 hours

Ingredients

- 3/4 cup whole wheat flour
- 1/4 teaspoon baking soda
- 1/4 cup cocoa powder
- 1/8 teaspoon salt
- 1/2 (12 oz.) package silken tofu, drained
- 1/4 cup olive oil
- 1 cup white sugar
- 4 teaspoons vanilla extract
- 4 (1 oz.) squares bittersweet chocolate, chopped
- 1/2 cup dark chocolate chips

Instructions

1. Preheat an oven to 350 degrees F (175 degrees C). Grease an 8-inch square pan.
2. Combine flour, baking soda, cocoa powder, and salt in a bowl.
3. Place the tofu in a blender and puree until smooth. Add olive oil and sugar. Blend for another minute. Pour into a mixing bowl and stir in the vanilla extract.
4. Simmer and melt the chocolate in a pot, stirring frequently with a rubber spatula. Mix the melted chocolate into the tofu mixture until well blended. Add in and stir flour mixture until thoroughly combined, about 3 minutes. Fold in the chocolate chips.
5. Bake in the preheated oven, about 30 minutes until a toothpick inserted into the center comes out clean. Cool. Cut into squares and serve.

Raw Brownies
SERVINGS: 9
PREP/TOTAL TIME: 10 min.

Ingredients

- 1 cup raisins
- 1 cup almonds
- 1/4 cup cocoa powder

Instructions

1. Blend raisins, almonds, and cocoa powder in a blender until it turns doughy.
2. Press dough into an 8 x 8 pan.
3. Cut into squares and serve.

Tofu Fudge Mocha Bars

SERVINGS: 24
PREP TIME: 5 min.
TOTAL TIME: 15 min.

Ingredients

- 1 (12 oz.) package silken tofu, undrained
- 2 tablespoons safflower oil
- 1 pinch salt
- 2 ⅓ cups turbinado sugar
- 1 cup cocoa powder
- 1/3 cup instant decaffeinated coffee powder
- 1 teaspoon vanilla extract
- 1 cup whole wheat flour

Instructions

1. Preheat oven to 325 degrees F (165 degrees C).
2. Blend tofu until creamy using a mixer or blender. Add and blend oil, salt, sugar, cocoa, coffee and vanilla.
3. Remove the bowl from the mixer or blender when sugar is dissolved into the tofu mixture and whisk in flour.
4. Pour batter into a greased 9 x 13-inch baking pan.
5. Bake 25 to 30 minutes, or until the cake pulls away from the side of the pan. Cool in the pan. Cut and serve

Walnut Brownies

SERVINGS: 20
PREP TIME: 20 min.
TOTAL TIME: 45 min.

Ingredients

- 1/3 cup all-purpose flour
- 1 cup water
- 1/2 cup butter
- 2/3 cup unsweetened cocoa powder
- 2 cups white sugar
- 1 teaspoon vanilla extract
- 2 cups all-purpose flour
- 2½ teaspoons baking powder
- 1/2 teaspoon salt
- 1/2 cup chopped walnuts

Instructions

1. Preheat oven to 350 degrees F (175 degrees C). Grease a 9 x 13-inch pan.
2. Combine flour and water in a saucepan. Cook over medium heat, stirring constantly until thick. Transfer to a mixing bowl, set aside, and cool.
3. Melt butter in a small saucepan. When butter has melted, add the cocoa and mix until smooth. Set aside to cool.
4. Beat the sugar and vanilla into the cooled flour mixture with an electric beater. Stir in and blend the cocoa mixture. Combine the flour, baking powder and salt, stir into the batter until blended. Fold in walnuts. Spread dough evenly in the prepared pan.
5. Bake in the preheated oven, for 20 to 25 minutes or until a toothpick inserted into the center comes out clean. Cool. Cut into squares and serve.

PUDDINGS

Avocado, Banana & Chocolate Pudding

SERVINGS: 6
PREP TIME: 10 min.
TOTAL TIME: 1 hour 10 min

Ingredients

- 1 ripe avocado, peeled and pitted
- 4 very ripe bananas
- 1/4 cup unsweetened cocoa powder, plus more for garnish

Instructions

1. In a blender, blend avocados, bananas, and cocoa powder until smooth.
2. Pour into serving bowls and sprinkle additional cocoa powder on top.
3. Chill in refrigerator for at least 1 hour. Serve.

Chocolate Pudding
SERVINGS: 4
PREP TIME: 5 min.
TOTAL TIME: 3 hours 30 min

Ingredients

- 2 tablespoons cornstarch
- 1 cup soy milk
- 1 cup soy creamer
- 1/2 cup white sugar
- 3 tablespoons egg replacer (dry)
- 3 oz. semisweet chocolate, chopped
- 2 teaspoons vanilla extract

Instructions

1. In a medium saucepan mix in cornstarch, soy milk and soy creamer. Stir until cornstarch is dissolved. Place on medium heat and stir in sugar. Whisking frequently until mixture begins to boil. Remove from heat.
2. In a small bowl whisk egg replacer with 1/4 cup of hot milk mixture. Return to pan with remaining milk mixture. Cook over medium heat for 3 to 4 minutes, until thick. Make sure it is not boiling.
3. Place the chocolate in a medium bowl and pour in the hot milk mixture. Let stand for 30 seconds and stir until melted and smooth. Cool for 10 to 15 minutes. Stir in vanilla.
4. Pour into custard cups. Cover with plastic wrap and let cool at room temperature. Refrigerate for 3 hours or overnight.

Whipped Coconut Cream

SERVINGS: 4
PREP TIME: 10 min.
TOTAL TIME: 8 hours 10 min.

Ingredients

- 1 (14 oz.) can unsweetened coconut milk
- 2 tablespoons white sugar, or to taste
- 1 teaspoon pure vanilla extract

Instructions

1. Refrigerate a can of coconut milk overnight.
2. Before making whipped cream, place metal mixing bowl and beaters in the refrigerator or freezer for 1 hour.
3. Open can of coconut milk, without shaking it. Scoop coconut cream solids into cold mixing bowl. Reserve remaining liquid.
4. Beat coconut cream using electric mixer with chilled beaters on medium speed and then turn to high speed. Continue beating 7 to 8 minutes or until stiff peaks form. Add sugar and vanilla extract and beat another minute. Taste and add more sugar if desired.

Raw Chocolate Pudding

SERVINGS: 4
PREP TIME: 10 min.
TOTAL TIME: 1 hour 10 min

Ingredients

- 1 avocado-peeled, pitted, and cut into chunks
- 1 banana, peeled and cut into chunks
- 1 cup unsweetened soy milk
- 1/4 cup raw cocoa powder
- 2 tablespoons agave nectar
- 1 teaspoon lemon juice
- 1/4 cup shredded unsweetened coconut (optional)

Instructions

1. Place avocado, banana, soy milk, cocoa powder, agave nectar, lemon juice, and coconut into a blender. Cover. Puree until smooth.
2. Divide into small containers, and store in the refrigerator for at least 1 hour or until set.

Vegan Carrot Pudding
SERVINGS: 4
PREP TIME: 10 min.
TOTAL TIME: 45 min.

Ingredients

- 1 cup vanilla soy milk
- 2 tablespoons turbinado sugar
- 1½ teaspoons blackstrap molasses
- 1 teaspoon vanilla extract
- 1/2 teaspoon ground cinnamon
- 1/4 teaspoon ground ginger
- 1/4 teaspoon ground allspice
- 1/8 teaspoon ground nutmeg
- 2 tablespoons all-purpose flour
- 1/3 cup raisins
- 1/3 cup chopped walnuts
- 2 cups shredded carrots

Instructions

1. In a saucepan over medium-low heat, whisk soy milk, turbinado sugar, molasses, vanilla extract, cinnamon, ginger, allspice, and nutmeg until well incorporated, 2 to 3 minutes. Whisk in flour another 3 to 5 minutes until smooth.
2. Fold raisins and walnuts into soy milk mixture. Add carrots. Cook and stir pudding over low heat, keeping from boiling, until carrots are softened, around 30 minutes.

Chocolate Pudding 2

SERVINGS: 2
PREP TIME: 10 min.
TOTAL TIME: 45 min.

Ingredients

- 3 tablespoons cornstarch
- 2 tablespoons water
- 1½ cups soy milk
- 1/4 teaspoon vanilla extract
- 1/4 cup white sugar
- 1/4 cup unsweetened cocoa powder

Instructions

1. In small bowl, form a paste by combining cornstarch and water.
2. In large saucepan over medium heat, stir soy milk, vanilla, sugar, cocoa and cornstarch mixture. Stir constantly until mixture boils and continue to stir until it thickens. Remove from heat.
3. Allow to cool five minutes and thicken. Chill in refrigerator until completely cool.
4. Serve.

Quinoa Pudding
SERVINGS: 6
PREP TIME: 5 min.
TOTAL TIME: 40 min.

Ingredients

- 1 cup quinoa
- 2 cups water
- 2 cups apple juice
- 1 cup raisins
- 2 tablespoons lemon juice
- 1 teaspoon ground cinnamon, or to taste
- salt to taste
- 2 teaspoons vanilla extract

Instructions

1. Place quinoa in a sieve and thoroughly rinse. Drain then place in a medium saucepan with water. Over high heat, bring to a boil. Lower heat, cover the pan with lid, and simmer about 15 minutes or until all water is absorbed and quinoa is soft.
2. Add and mix in apple juice, raisins, lemon juice, cinnamon, and salt. Cover pan and simmer for 15 more minutes. Stir in vanilla extract. Serve warm.

Chocolate Avocado Pudding

SERVINGS: 4
PREP TIME: 10 min.
TOTAL TIME: 40 min.

Ingredients

- 2 large avocados-peeled, pitted, and cubed
- 1/2 cup unsweetened cocoa powder
- 1/2 cup brown sugar
- 1/3 cup coconut milk
- 2 teaspoons vanilla extract
- 1 pinch ground cinnamon

Instructions

1. In a blender, combine and blend avocados, cocoa powder, brown sugar, coconut milk, vanilla extract, and cinnamon until smooth.
2. Refrigerate pudding, about 30 minutes or until chilled.

<u>*PIES*</u>

Roasted Papaya with Brown Sugar Pie
SERVINGS: 4
PREP/ TOTAL TIME: 1 hour

Ingredients

- 2 tablespoons light-brown sugar
- 1/4 teaspoon ground ginger
- 2 medium Solo papayas (14 oz. each), halved lengthwise and seeded
- 1/4 teaspoon cayenne pepper
- 1 lime, cut into 4 wedges

Instructions

1. Preheat oven to 450 degrees (230 degrees C).
2. Stir and mix sugar and ginger in a small bowl.
3. Arrange papaya halves, cut sides up, in a 10-by-13-inch baking dish. Sprinkle sugar mixture evenly over papaya.
4. Bake in the oven, around 35 to 40 minutes, brushing papaya with melted sugar mixture 2 or 3 times until papaya edges darken and mixture is bubbling.
5. Sprinkle each serving with a pinch of cayenne.
6. Serve with lime wedges.

Blackberry Pie

SERVINGS: 8
PREP /TOTAL TIME: 1 hour

Ingredients

- 2¼ cups all-purpose flour
- 1 teaspoon salt
- 1/2 cup vegetable oil
- 3 tablespoons cold water
- 2/3 cup white sugar
- 1/2 teaspoon ground cinnamon
- 3 cups fresh blackberries

Instructions

1. Preheat oven to 425 degrees F (220 degrees C).
2. Mix 2 cups flour and salt in a medium mixing bowl. Make a dent in the center and pour in the oil and water. Mix together.
3. Separate the dough into two balls, using 3/4 of the dough for the first ball and 1/4 of the dough for the second. Place a sheet of wax paper over the bigger ball of dough, and roll it out (the wax paper will keep the dough in one large piece). Line an 8-inch pie pan with the dough. Roll out the small ball of dough similarly, and set aside.
4. In a small bowl, mix sugar, 1/4 cup flour, and cinnamon. Place the berries in a large bowl, and sprinkle sugar mixture over them. Gently stir to coat. Spread the filling into the dough lined pie pan. Cover with the rest of the dough, and pinch the crusts together. Poke holes in the top to allow steam to escape during baking. Line the edges of the crust with tin foil.
5. Bake in preheated oven for 30 to 45 minutes, or until crust is lightly browned and filling is hot and bubbly. Let cool.

Tofu Chocolate Pie

Ingredients

- 1 pound silken tofu
- 1/2 cup unsweetened cocoa powder
- 1 cup white sugar
- 1 tablespoon vanilla extract
- 1/2 teaspoon cider vinegar
- 1 (9 inch) prepared graham cracker crust

Instructions

1. Preheat oven to 375 degrees F (190 degrees C).
2. Blend tofu with an electric mixer or blender until smooth. Add and blend in cocoa, sugar, vanilla and vinegar. Pour into prepared crust.
3. Bake in preheated oven for 25 minutes.
4. Refrigerate for an hour before serving.

Tofu Pumpkin Pie
SERVINGS: 8
PREP TIME: 5 min.
TOTAL TIME: 2 hours

Ingredients

- 1 (10.5 oz.) package silken tofu, drained
- 1 (16 oz.) can pumpkin puree
- 3/4 cup white sugar
- 1/2 teaspoon salt
- 1 teaspoon ground cinnamon
- 1/2 teaspoon ground ginger
- 1/4 teaspoon ground cloves
- 1 (9 inch) unbaked pie crust

Instructions

1. Preheat an oven to 450 degrees F.
2. Place the tofu, pumpkin, sugar, salt, cinnamon, ginger, and clove into a blender. Blend until smooth. Pour into the pie crust.
3. Bake in the preheated oven 15 minutes. Reduce heat to 350 degrees F and continue baking about more 40 minutes until a knife inserted into the mixture comes out clean. Cool before serving.

CANDY

Orange and Lemon Peel Candy

SERVINGS: 12
PREP TIME: 10 min.
TOTAL TIME: 4 hours 40 min

Ingredients

- 6 lemon peels, cut into 1/4 inch strips
- 4 orange peels, cut into 1/4 inch strips
- 2 cups white sugar
- 1 cup water
- 1/3 cup white sugar

Instructions

1. In large saucepan, add the lemon and orange peels and cover with water. Boil over high heat for 20 minutes. Drain and set aside.
2. Combine 2 cups sugar and 1 cup of water in medium saucepan. Bring to a boil and cook until mixture reaches, 230 degrees F (108 degrees C), or when a small amount dropped in cold water forms a soft thread. Add and stir in peel, reduce heat. Simmer 5 minutes and stir frequently. Drain.
3. Roll peel pieces, a couple at a time, in remaining sugar. Dry on wire rack for several hours. Store in airtight container.

Raw Candy
SERVINGS: 40
PREP/TOTAL TIME: 20 min.

Ingredients

- 1 cup raisins
- 1 cup walnuts
- 1 tablespoon vegetable oil
- 1 cup sliced almonds

Instructions

1. In a blender or food processor blend raisins and walnuts together until they form a sticky ball.
2. Coat your hands with oil and roll the mixture into marble sized balls. Coat with sliced almonds.
3. Cover and refrigerate up to 3 days.

Candied Apples

SERVINGS: 15
PREP TIME: 10 min.
TOTAL TIME: 40 min.

Ingredients

- 15 apples
- 2 cups white sugar
- 1 cup light corn syrup
- 1½ cups water
- 8 drops red food coloring

Instructions

1. Grease cookie sheets. Insert craft sticks into whole, stemmed apples.
2. In a medium saucepan combine sugar, corn syrup and water over medium-high heat. Heat to 300 degrees F (150 degrees C), or until a small amount of syrup dropped into cold water forms hard and brittle threads. Remove from heat and stir in food coloring.
3. Hold apple by its stick, dip in syrup and turn to coat evenly. Place on prepared sheets until hardened.

Rock Candy
SERVINGS: 24
PREP TIME: 20 min.
TOTAL TIME: 10 days

Ingredients

- 6 cups cold water
- 6 cups white sugar

Instructions

1. Place water in a large bowl. Gradually add and dissolve the sugar in the water, stirring until sugar is completely dissolved. Pour sugar water into clean jar and place a wooden skewer in the jar, making sure the top sticks out from the water. Cover with a cloth, and place jar in a cool place away from bright lights. Do not disturb the crystals and leave it for several days until all water is evaporated and crystals have formed on the skewer.

Coconut Ice

SERVINGS: 20
PREP TIME: 5 min.
TOTAL TIME: 1 hour 30 min

Ingredients

- 2 cups white sugar
- 2/3 cup water
- 1 teaspoon vanilla extract
- 1 ⅓ cups flaked coconut
- 2 drops red food coloring

Instructions

1. Line a 7 x 7 inch pan with waxed paper or parchment. In a medium saucepan, combine and heat sugar and water on medium heat until sugar has dissolved. Bring to a boil and cook until it reaches 240 degrees F (120 degrees C), or a when syrup dropped in a glass of cold water forms a soft ball.
2. Remove from heat and immediately add and stir in vanilla and coconut. Stir 5 to 10 minutes or until mixture begins to thicken.
3. Pour half of the mixture into the prepared pan and with a knife or spatula, level the surface. Stir in the food coloring to the other half of the mixture. Pour the pink mixture on top of other layer, and level the surface. With the back of a spoon, press all down firmly and allow to harden. When firm, turn out of the pan, remove the paper and cut into squares.

FROZEN DESSERTS

Pineapple and Basil Sorbet
SERVINGS: 16
PREP TIME: 20 min.
TOTAL TIME: 9 hours 20 min.

Ingredients

- 1 pineapple-peeled, cored, and cut into chunks
- 1/2 cup white sugar
- 1/2 cup pineapple juice
- 1/4 cup basil leaves

Instructions

1. In a blender, blend pineapple, sugar, pineapple juice, and basil until smooth. Refrigerate for 1 hour.
2. Place mixture in an ice cream maker and mix according to manufacturer's instructions. Or alternatively, pour the mixture into a container, and freeze 3 to 4 hours or until solid. Thoroughly stir the sorbet breaking up the ice crystals into a slushy consistency, and return to freezer until firm, about 3 hours.
3. Store in the freezer in a covered container. Freeze overnight.

Pink Grapefruit Blueberry Sorbet

SERVINGS: 10
PREP TIME: 5 min.
TOTAL TIME: 6 hours 5 min.

Ingredients

- 3 cups fresh pink grapefruit juice
- 3 cups fresh or frozen blueberries
- 1½ cups white sugar, or to taste

Instructions

1. In a blender, pour grapefruit juice, blueberries, and sugar. Blend 2 to 3 minutes or until the sugar is dissolved and mixture is smooth.
2. Pour mixture into a container, and freeze 3 to 4 hours or until solid. Stir the sorbet to a slushy consistency, and return to freezer about 3 hours or until firm.
3. Pour into an airtight container. Freeze overnight.

Soda Pop Ice Cream

SERVINGS: 2
PREP/TOTAL TIME: 5 min.

Ingredients

- 1½ cups snow
- 3/4 (12 oz.) can cola-flavored carbonated beverage

Instructions

1. In a medium bowl, combine and stir snow and cola.
2. Serve immediately.

Mint-Grapefruit Granita
SERVINGS: 4
PREP TIME: 20 min.
TOTAL TIME: 6 hours 20 min.

Ingredients

- 1/2 cup sugar
- 1/4 cup packed fresh mint leaves, plus more for garnish
- 2 cups fresh grapefruit juice (about 3 medium grapefruits), strained
- 1/4 cup fresh lemon juice (about 2 lemons), strained

Instructions

1. In a small saucepan, combine sugar, mint, and 1/2 cup water. Bring to a boil over medium-high heat, and stir often until sugar dissolves, about 3 to 5 minutes.
2. In a blender, combine fruit juices and mint syrup. Puree for 30 seconds on high. Pour into a shallow 2-quart baking dish. Freeze overnight or until solid.
3. Break granita into large chunks with a fork. Pulse in a food processor to form small crystals.
4. Serve immediately, with mint leaves, or cover and freeze up to 2 hours.

Lime & Basil Sorbet

SERVINGS: 8
PREP TIME: 30 min.
TOTAL TIME: 2 hours 35 min.

Ingredients

- 1 cup sugar
- 1 cup water
- 3/4 cup fresh lime juice
- 20 fresh basil leaves, minced

Instructions

1. In a medium saucepan, bring water and sugar to a simmer over medium high heat until sugar is dissolved. Remove from heat.
2. Combine and puree syrup, lime juice, and basil in a blender. Pour the mixture in a container. Cover and store in freezer about 2 hours or until completely frozen.
3. Break frozen mixture into pieces and place in the blender. Blend until smooth. Return to the container and cover.
4. Store in freezer until ready to serve.

Frozen Tropical Fruit Salad

SERVINGS: 6
PREP TIME: 15 min.
TOTAL TIME: 1 hour 15 min.

Ingredients

- 1/2 cup white sugar
- 2 cups water
- 1 (6 oz.) can frozen orange juice concentrate, thawed
- 1 (6 oz.) can frozen lemonade concentrate, thawed
- 4 bananas, sliced
- 1 (20 oz.) can crushed pineapple with juice
- 1 (10 oz.) package frozen strawberries, thawed

Instructions

1. Dissolve sugar in the water. Add orange juice, lemonade, bananas, crushed pineapple with juice, strawberries and mix.
2. Pour into 9 x13 inch glass pan. Freeze until solid. When ready to serve, let it sit out for about 5 minutes before attempting to cut.

Pineapple Orange Sorbet
SERVINGS: 10
PREP TIME: 20 min.
TOTAL TIME: 3 hours

Ingredients

- 1/2 cup water
- 1/2 cup granulated sugar
- 2 cups orange juice
- 1 tablespoon lemon juice
- 1 (20 oz.) can crushed pineapple
- 2 teaspoons freshly grated orange zest

Instructions

1. In a medium saucepan, bring water and sugar over medium high heat to a simmer until sugar is dissolved.
2. Puree pineapple with its juice until smooth in a food processor or blender. Transfer to a metal bowl, and stir in syrup, lemon juice, orange juice, and orange zest. Freeze until slightly firm, but not completely frozen.
3. Process mixture in the food processor or blend in a blender until smooth.
4. Transfer to a container and freeze about 2 hours or until firm. Serve.

Peach and Strawberry Sorbet

SERVINGS: 4
PREP TIME: 15 min.
TOTAL TIME: 3 hours 15 min.

Ingredients

- 2 cups sliced fresh peaches
- 1 cup fresh strawberries, hulled
- 1 cup fresh orange juice
- 1/4 cup brown sugar

Instructions

1. Place peaches, strawberries, orange juice, and brown sugar in a food processor. Puree until smooth.
2. Pour mixture into an ice cream maker and freeze according to manufacturer's instructions until firm. Or alternatively, cover and store in freezer about 2 hours or until completely frozen.
3. Break frozen mixture into pieces and place in the blender. Blend until smooth. Return to the container and cover.
4. Store in freezer until ready to serve.

Coconut-Lime Sorbet

SERVINGS: 4
PREP/TOTAL TIME: 30 min.

Ingredients

- 1 (15 oz.) can cream of coconut
- 1/2 cup fresh lime juice
- 3/4 cup water

Instructions

1. Combine the cream of coconut, lime juice, and water in the container of an ice cream maker. Freeze according to manufacturer's instructions.
2. Alternatively, combine and puree the cream of coconut, lime juice, and water in a blender. Pour the mixture in a container. Cover and store in freezer about 2 hours or until completely frozen.
3. Break frozen mixture into pieces and place in the blender. Blend until smooth. Return to the container and cover.
4. Store in freezer until ready to serve.

Banana Ice Cream

SERVINGS: 2
PREP/ TOTAL TIME: 10 min.

Ingredients

- 2 large frozen bananas, cut into small chunks
- 1 cup unsweetened almond milk
- 1 tablespoon chopped pecans
- 1 pinch ground cinnamon, or to taste

Instructions

1. Blend bananas, almond milk, pecans, and cinnamon together in a blender or food processor until creamy and smooth.

Chocolate-Hazelnut Soy Ice Cream

SERVINGS: 4
PREP TIME: 10 min.
TOTAL TIME: 6 hours 10 min.

Ingredients

- 1/2 (12 oz.) package extra-firm silken tofu
- 1 cup soy milk
- 1 tablespoon hazelnut flavored syrup
- 4 teaspoons instant espresso powder
- 1 teaspoon vanilla extract
- 2/3 cup semisweet chocolate chips, melted

Instructions

1. In a blender, combine tofu, soy milk, hazelnut syrup, espresso powder, and vanilla extract. Cover and puree until smooth. Pour in the melted chocolate, and puree until evenly mixed. Pour the mixture into a bowl and cover. Refrigerate at least 1 hour or until cold.
2. Pour the cold mixture into an ice cream maker and freeze according to the manufacturer's directions.
3. When ice cream has thickened, remove it from the ice cream maker and transfer it to a container. Freeze 4 hours or overnight before serving.

Cranberry Ice

SERVINGS: 12
PREP/TOTAL TIME: 45 min.

Ingredients

- 2 (12 oz.) packages fresh cranberries
- 2 cups white sugar
- 1¼ cups fresh orange juice
- 1 cup fresh lemon juice

Instructions

1. In a large pot, add cranberries and enough water to cover. Boil until cranberries begin to pop. Drain and put through a food mill placed over a large bowl.
2. While still warm add sugar to dissolve in the warm berries. The amount of sugar may vary depending on the tartness of the berries, so if you decide to add more sugar remember that the mixture will be tarter when it has been frozen.
3. After dissolving the sugar in the berries, stir in fresh squeezed orange juice and fresh squeezed lemon juice. Pour in 8 or 9-inch square pan and freeze overnight. Take out of the freezer 5-10 minutes before cutting.

Watermelon Granita with Champagne

SERVINGS: 4
PREP TIME: 15 min.
TOTAL TIME: 2 hours 15 min.

Ingredients

- 2 pounds watermelon, seeded and cubed
- 1/2 cup white sugar
- 1 cup champagne
- 4 slices watermelon

Instructions

1. Place cubed watermelon and sugar in a blender. Blend for 1 minute. Stir in the champagne. Pour this mixture into a plastic container. Cover and place in the freezer. Stir mixture with a fork every 30 minutes until frozen, for about 2 hours.
2. Before serving, remove the frozen granita from the freezer and stir well using a fork or process in the food processor until the desired consistency is reached.
3. Serve in tall glasses garnished with sliced watermelon.

FRUIT SALADS & SOUPS

Strawberry Salad with Balsamic Vinegar

SERVINGS: 6
PREP TIME: 10 min.
TOTAL TIME: 1 hour 10 min.

Ingredients

- 16 oz. fresh strawberries, hulled and large berries cut in half
- 2 tablespoons balsamic vinegar
- 1/4 cup white sugar
- 1/4 teaspoon freshly ground black pepper, or to taste

Instructions

1. Place strawberries in a bowl and drizzle vinegar over strawberries. Sprinkle with sugar. Stir gently. Cover, and let sit at room temperature for between 1 and 4 hours.
2. Grind pepper over berries before serving.

Watercress, Melon and Almond Salad

Ingredients

- 3 tablespoons fresh lime juice
- 1 teaspoon white sugar
- 1 teaspoon minced fresh ginger root
- 1/4 cup vegetable oil
- 2 bunches watercress, trimmed and chopped
- 2½ cups cubed watermelon
- 2½ cups cubed cantaloupe
- 1/3 cup toasted and sliced almonds

Instructions

1. In a large bowl, whisk together lime juice, sugar, and ginger. Gradually add oil and season with salt and pepper.
2. Add watercress, watermelon, and cantaloupe to dressing. Toss to coat.
3. Transfer salad to plates. Sprinkle with sliced almonds.
4. Serve immediately.

Frozen Berries Soup Salad
SERVINGS: 5
PREP/TOTAL TIME: 2 hours.

Ingredients

- 1/2 cup barley
- 6 cups water
- 1/2 cup white sugar
- 1 (10 oz.) package frozen raspberries
- 1/2 cup raisins
- 1 cup pitted cherries

Instructions

1. In a large bowl, soak the barley overnight in the water.
2. In a large saucepan simmer the barley for 1 hour over low heat. Add sugar, raspberries and raisins and simmer for another 30 minutes. Add cherries and simmer for another 15 minutes or until the soup becomes thick.
3. Chill in the refrigerator and serve cold.

Strawberry Tapioca

SERVINGS: 4
PREP TIME: 10 min.
TOTAL TIME: 30 min.

Ingredients

- 1/2 cup fresh strawberries, hulled and halved
- 1½ cups water
- 1/4 cup quick-cooking tapioca

Instructions

1. In a food processor or in a blender blend strawberries and water until smooth. Pour into a small saucepan. Add and stir in tapioca. Let stand for 10 minutes or until softened. Bring to a boil over medium heat, stir frequently to prevent sticking. Remove when thick and pour into serving dishes.

Elderberry Soup

SERVINGS: 4
PREP TIME: 25 min.
TOTAL TIME: 45 min.

Ingredients

- 5 oz. elderberries
- 1-quart water, divided
- 1½ teaspoons cornstarch
- 1/2 pound apples-peeled, cored and diced
- 1 lemon peel
- white sugar to taste

Instructions

1. In a pot, place elderberries with 2 cups water and bring to a boil. Reduce heat to low and simmer 10 minutes. Remove from heat, puree in a blender until smooth. Return to the pot. In a small bowl, mix the cornstarch with 1 tablespoon of the puree, and stir back into the pot to thicken.
2. In a separate pot, bring the apples and remaining water to a boil. Place the lemon peel in the pot. Reduce heat to low and simmer 10 minutes. Remove the lemon peel. Mix the elderberry puree into the apple mixture. Sweeten to taste with sugar.

Spicy Melon Soup

SERVINGS: 4
PREP/TOTAL TIME: 15 min.

Ingredients

- 4 cups casaba melon, seeded and cubed
- 3/4 cup coconut milk
- 2 lime juice
- 1 tablespoon freshly grated ginger
- 1 pinch salt

Instructions

1. In a food processor, combine casaba melon, coconut milk, lime juice, ginger, and salt. Process for 1 to 2 minutes or until the mixture is smooth.
2. Serve.

SNACKS & APPETIZERS

Spiced Plantains and Pineapple
SERVINGS: 4
PREP TIME: 5 min.
TOTAL TIME: 10 min.

Ingredients

- 2 ripe plantains (yellow and black skin), peeled and cut into 1 inch rounds
- 1 (20 oz.) can pineapple chunks in juice, drained, juice reserved
- 1 teaspoon ground cinnamon
- 3/4 teaspoon ground nutmeg
- 3/4 teaspoon ground cloves

Instructions

1. Heat a large skillet over medium heat and coat with cooking spray. Arrange plantain slices on the skillet in a single layer. Season with half of the cinnamon, nutmeg and cloves. Cook 2 to 3 minutes or until golden brown on the bottom. Turn over the slices and pour in the pineapple and a small amount of the juice. Sprinkle the remaining spices over the top and cook another 3 minutes or until browned on the bottom.

Orange Poached Pears
SERVINGS: 3
PREP TIME: 15 min.
TOTAL TIME: 1 hour 45 min.

Ingredients

- 1½ cups orange juice without pulp
- 1/2 cup packed brown sugar
- 1/4 cup white sugar
- 1 tablespoon vanilla extract
- 1 teaspoon ground cinnamon
- 3 whole pears, peeled and cored
- 1/2 cup chopped walnuts

Instructions

1. In a large saucepan mix together the orange juice, brown and white sugar, vanilla extract, and cinnamon over medium heat. Bring to a boil, and stir until sugar is dissolved. Place pears in syrup, and cover. Simmer pears for 1 hour and 15 minutes, while spooning sauce every 10 minutes over pears, and turning pears twice.
2. Transfer pears to individual serving dishes.
3. Continue cooking syrup, about 15 more minutes, constantly stirring until thickened. Mix in the walnuts.
4. Pour the sauce over the pears and serve.

Fried Cinnamon Strips

SERVINGS: 36
PREP TIME: 10 min.
TOTAL TIME: 30 min.

Ingredients

- 1 cup white sugar
- 1 teaspoon ground cinnamon
- 1/4 teaspoon ground nutmeg
- 10 (8 inch) flour tortillas
- 3 cups oil for frying

Instructions

1. Combine sugar, cinnamon and nutmeg in a large resealable plastic bag. Seal and toss to mix ingredients.
2. Heat oil in deep-fryer or deep skillet to 375 degrees F (190 degrees C). Fry for 30 seconds 4 or 5 tortilla strips on a side, until golden brown. Drain on paper towels.
3. While still warm, place the fried tortillas in bag and shake to coat with sugar mixture.
4. Serve immediately or store in an airtight container.

Chocolate-Covered Bananas

SERVINGS: 6
PREP TIME: 20 min.
TOTAL TIME: 40 min.

Ingredients

- 8 oz. semisweet chocolate, chopped
- 6 popsicle sticks or wooden skewers
- 2 bananas, peeled and cut crosswise into thirds
- 1/3 cup coarsely chopped salted peanuts

Instructions

1. Place chocolate in a heatproof bowl set over (not inside) a pan of simmering water. Stir until melted.
2. Line a baking sheet with waxed paper. Insert a Popsicle stick in one end of each banana piece. Dip bananas in chocolate, one at a time, and spoon on additional chocolate to cover.
3. Sprinkle bananas with peanuts, and set on prepared baking sheet.
4. Refrigerate at least 20 minutes, or until chocolate is firm.

Apple and Pumpkin Dessert
SERVINGS: 1
PREP TIME: 5 min.
TOTAL TIME: 9 min.

Ingredients

- 2 (1 gram) packets sugar substitute
- 1 teaspoon pumpkin pie spice
- 1 Granny Smith apple-peeled, cored and chopped
- 1/4 cup canned pumpkin
- 2 tablespoons water

Instructions

1. In the bottom of a microwave-safe bowl, sprinkle 1/3 packet of sugar substitute and 1/3 teaspoon pumpkin pie spice. Layer 1/4 of the apple pieces into the bowl and repeat. Spread the pumpkin over the apples. Sprinkle the remaining sugar substitute and pumpkin pie spice on the pumpkin. Top with the remaining apples.
2. Pour water over the mixture.
3. Cook in microwave on high for 3½ minutes, and stir every minute.

Baked Apples

SERVINGS: 1
PREP TIME: 5 min.
TOTAL TIME: 15 min

Ingredients

- 1 Granny Smith apple, cored
- 1 tablespoon brown sugar
- 1/4 teaspoon ground cinnamon

Instructions

1. Fill the core of the apple with the brown sugar and cinnamon. Wrap apple heavy foil, and twist extra foil into a tail for a handle.
2. Place apple in the coals of a campfire or barbeque and let cook 5 to 10 minutes, until softened. Alternatively, bake in preheated oven for 15 minutes, until sugar begins to caramelize and apples are tender
3. Remove and unwrap, be careful of burning yourself with the hot sugar.

Poached Mint Peaches
SERVINGS: 6
PREP/TOTAL TIME: 25 min.

Ingredients

- 6 firm, ripe peaches
- 2 cups sugar
- 1 vanilla bean, split (or 1/2 teaspoon pure vanilla extract)
- 2 strips lemon zest
- 1 large mint sprig, plus more for serving
- 4 cups water

Instructions

1. Lightly carve an X into bottom of peaches using a paring knife. In a large saucepan, combine sugar, vanilla, lemon zest, mint, and water. Cook over medium heat, about 2 minutes or until sugar has dissolved, stirring occasionally.
2. Add peaches and cover with water. Barely simmer for about 6 to 10 minutes, turning occasionally, until peaches are soft enough to easily pierce with a skewer.
3. Remove peaches and let slightly cool. Peel peaches using a paring knife and return to syrup.
4. Serve with mint sprigs.

Date Charoset

SERVINGS: 40
PREP TIME: 45 min.
TOTAL TIME: 2 hours 15 min.

Ingredients

- 1/2 pound chopped dates
- 1 cup golden raisins
- 1/2 cup red wine
- 1/2 cup coarsely chopped walnuts
- 1 teaspoon ground cinnamon
- 1/2 cup confectioners' sugar

Instructions

1. In a small saucepan, combine dates, raisins, and wine. Cook over low heat, and stir occasionally, until fruit thickens to a soft paste. Cool.
2. Stir nuts and cinnamon into the fruit mixture.
3. Form paste into small, bite-size balls. Roll in confectioners' sugar.
4. Serve.

Coconut Date Bars
SERVINGS: 4
PREP TIME: 10 min.
TOTAL TIME: 40 min.

Ingredients

- 1/3 cup slivered almonds
- 1/2 cup flaked coconut
- 10 pitted dates
- 1/4 cup cashews
- 1 teaspoon coconut oil

Instructions

1. Blend almonds and coconut in a food processor. Add dates and pulse until combined. Add cashews and coconut oil, pulsing until mixture is thick and sticks together.
2. Transfer to a sheet of waxed paper. Form into a square and fold sides of waxed paper over the top.
3. Refrigerate at least 30 minutes or until solid.

Fried Plantains
SERVINGS: 8
PREP TIME: 5 min.
TOTAL TIME: 15 min.

Ingredients

- 1-quart oil for frying
- 2 plantains

Instructions

1. Preheat oil in a large deep skillet over medium high heat.
2. Peel the plantains and cut them in half. Slice the halves lengthwise into thin pieces.
3. Fry the pieces until tender and browned. Drain excess oil on paper towels.

Cherry Crisp

Ingredients

- 1 (21 oz.) can cherry pie filling
- 1/2 cup all-purpose flour
- 1/2 cup rolled oats
- 2/3 cup brown sugar
- 3/4 teaspoon ground cinnamon
- 3/4 teaspoon ground nutmeg
- 1/4 cup chopped pecans
- 1/3 cup melted margarine

Instructions

1. Preheat oven to 350 degrees F (175 degrees C.) Lightly grease a 2-quart baking dish. Pour pie filling into the dish, spreading evenly.
2. Combine flour, oats, sugar, cinnamon, and nutmeg in a medium bowl. Add melted margarine and mix. Spread over pie filling, and sprinkle with chopped pecans.
3. Bake in preheated oven for 30 minutes or until topping is golden brown.
4. Cool 15 minutes before serving.

Thai Fried Bananas

SERVINGS: 20
PREP TIME: 20 min.
TOTAL TIME: 35 min.

Ingredients

- 3/4 cup white rice flour
- 1/4 cup tapioca flour
- 2 tablespoons white sugar
- 1 teaspoon salt
- 1/2 cup shredded coconut
- 1¼ cups water
- 10 bananas
- 3 cups oil for frying

Instructions

1. In a medium bowl, combine rice flour, tapioca, sugar, salt and coconut. Gradually stir in water and mix to form a thick batter.
2. Peel the bananas and cut each lengthwise into 3 or 4 pieces. Heat oil in deep-fryer or deep wok to 375 degrees F (190 degrees C).
3. Coat each banana slice completely in batter. Fry in hot oil, turning until golden on both sides.
4. Drain on paper towels. Serve immediately.

Sweet Sticky Rice with Mangoes

SERVINGS: 6
PREP TIME: 15 min.
TOTAL TIME: 1 hour 35 min.

Ingredients

- 2 cups uncooked glutinous (sticky) white rice, rinsed
- 1 (13.5 oz.) can coconut milk, divided
- 1 cup white sugar
- 1 tablespoon white sugar
- 1/4 teaspoon salt
- 3/4 teaspoon cornstarch
- 2 ripe mangoes, peeled and cubed

Instructions

1. Cover rice with several inches of fresh water. Stand for 30 minutes. Drain so rice is covered by only 1/4 inch of water.
2. Place rice in a microwave oven, cover, and cook on High for about 10 minutes or until the water has been absorbed and the rice is still wet. Stir and cook an additional 4 minutes or until almost dry.
3. Mix half the coconut milk and 1 cup of sugar in a bowl and stir to dissolve the sugar. Pour mixture over rice and stir until rice is coated with the mixture. Cover and allow the rice to stand at room temperature for 20 minutes.
4. Pour remaining 1/2 can of coconut milk into a saucepan and whisk in 1 tablespoon of sugar, salt, and cornstarch until smooth. Bring mixture to a simmer about 2 minutes over medium heat, constantly whisk, until thickened. Remove from heat and cool.
5. Scoop the rice into individual serving bowls and top each with 2 tablespoons of the coconut sauce and mango pieces.

THANK YOU

Thank you for checking out my Vegan Desserts Cookbook. I hope you enjoyed these recipes as much as I have. I am always looking for feedback on how to improve, so if you have any questions, suggestions, or comments please send me an email at susan.evans.author@gmail.com. Also, if you enjoyed the book would you consider leaving on honest review? As a new author, they help me out in a big way. Thanks again, and have fun cooking!

Other popular books by Susan Evans

Vegetarian Slow Cooker Cookbook:
Over 75 recipes for meals, soups, stews, desserts, and sides

Quick & Easy Asian Vegetarian Cookbook:
Over 50 recipes for stir fries, rice, noodles, and appetizers

Vegetarian Mediterranean Cookbook:
Over 50 recipes for appetizers, salads, dips, and main dishes

Quick & Easy Vegetarian Rice Cooker Meals:
Over 50 recipes for breakfast, main dishes, and desserts

Quick & Easy Rice Cooker Meals:
Over 60 recipes for breakfast, main dishes, soups, and desserts

Quick & Easy Microwave Meals:
Over 50 recipes for breakfast, snacks, meals and desserts

Halloween Cookbook:
80 Ghoulish recipes for appetizers, meals, drinks, and desserts

Printed in Great Britain
by Amazon